HEALING MUDRAS
FOR YOUR BODY

VOLUME I.

NEW REVISED
FULL COLOR EDITION

SABRINA MESKO PH.D.H.

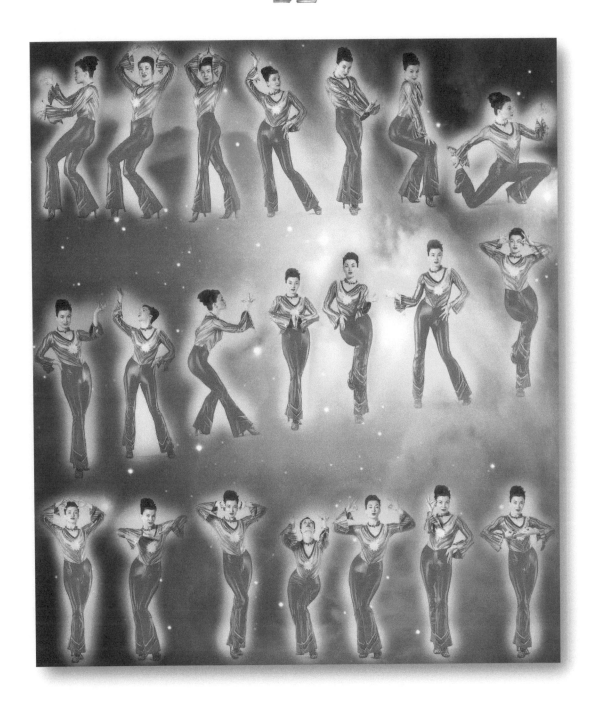

HEALING MUDRAS for BODY - Full Color Edition by Sabrina Mesko ~ 3

The material contained in this book is not intended as medical advice.
If you have a medical issue or illness, consult a qualified physician.

A Mudra Hands™ Book
Published by Mudra Hands Publishing

Photography by Dorothy Low
Illustrations by Kiar Mesko
Costume design, photo design, and styling by Sabrina Mesko
Cover photo by Dorothy Low
On The Cover ~ MUDRA for Preventing Burnout

Printed in the United States of America

ISBN-13: 978-0615811482
ISBN-10: 0615811485

Originally published by Random House in 2000
Under the title *Healing Mudras -Yoga for Your Hands*
New, revised, updated and expanded

To the greatest parents in the world,
Bibi and Kiar

By Sabrina Mesko

HEALING MUDRAS
Yoga for Your Hands
Random House - Original edition

POWER MUDRAS
Yoga Hand Postures for Women
Random House - Original edition

MUDRA - Gestures of POWER
DVD - Sounds True

CHAKRA MUDRAS DVD set
HAND YOGA for Vitality, Creativity and Success
HAND YOGA for Concentration, Love and Longevity

HEALING MUDRAS
Yoga for Your Hands - New Edition

HEALING MUDRAS - New Edition in full color:
Healing Mudras I. ~ For Your Body
Healing Mudras II. ~ For Your Mind
Healing Mudras III. ~ For Your Soul

POWER MUDRAS
Yoga Hand Postures for Women - New Edition

MUDRA THERAPY
Hand Yoga for Pain Management and Conquering Illness

YOGA MIND
45 Meditations for Inner Peace, Prosperity and Protection

MUDRAS for ASTROLOGICAL SIGNS
Volumes I. ~ XII.

MUDRAS for ARIES, TAURUS, GEMINI, CANCER, LEO, VIRGO, LIBRA, SCORPIO, SAGITTARIUS, CAPRICORN, AQUARIUS, PISCES
12 Book Series

LOVE MUDRAS
Hand Yoga for Two

MUDRAS AND CRYSTALS
The Alchemy of Energy Protection

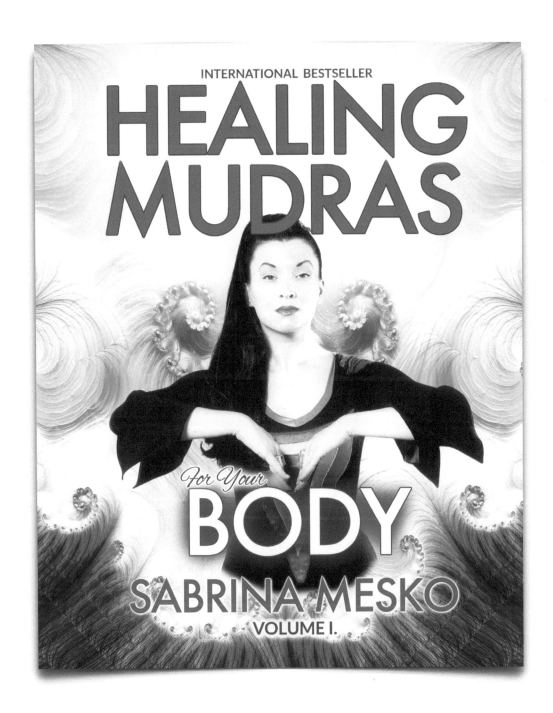

CONTENTS

MUDRAS FOR YOUR BODY

HEALING MUDRAS FOR YOUR BODY

YOGA FOR YOUR HANDS

Introduction

Mudras are the ancient sacred codes to your body, mind and spirit. They are a part of your everyday lives, intuitively used and intricately affecting your energy level, self-healing capacity and energy reception and output. The healing powers of Mudras are undeniable and needed now more than ever.

Thirteen years have passed since the original HEALING MUDRAS was published. As every author will tell you, the moment you let the book out of your hands, it begins a life of its own. Whether it is a long life or a short one, it depends on so many factors. HEALING MUDRAS is long-lived, for it has been translated into over 14 languages and has positively affected thousands of Mudra practitioners around the world. Since the first publication, I have traveled the globe, taught people these powerful ancient techniques in different languages, and received countless letters of gratitude for bringing Mudras into today's spotlight. Every time I receive a reader's letter, I am deeply joyful that another person has benefited from these techniques, and humbled for the opportunity of being a part of that process. I am only the messenger and instrument to convey these ancient sacred Mudras. It is truly a part of my life's mission and an honor to have had the pleasure of teaching Mudras to all kinds of audiences, all ages, all cultures, religions and spiritual convictions, or openness to healing aspects of such practices. I can honestly say that each and every person who practiced Mudras, has experienced the power magnitude of positive effects. It has been an amazing journey that continues to this day.

Mudras will always be a profound part of my life, and since the readers have asked me numerous times when my next project will be released, I have created a double DVD series titled Chakra Mudras to help expand available practice materials. And now the time has come for an updated NEW edition HEALING MUDRAS - a new revised version of the first book with the additional chapter. I have decided to offer the reader two choices; a complete book with black and white photographs, and a color version of the book in three separate volumes, for Body, Mind and Soul. The color edition was my original wish for the look and feel of the book and is now realized. What you hold in your hands is the Volume I. with full color photographs, nevertheless you, my dear reader, have the choice.

Thru the years passed I have often reflected on my destined meeting with my teacher Yogi Bhajan. I remain eternally grateful for everything he taught me and continue to follow every detail of his personal Mudra practice and teaching instructions.

My early years as a professional ballerina left within me a permanent imprint of discipline and persistence and I apply that to every aspect of my work with Mudras. They are such precise and intricate hand positions that need to be practiced with accuracy and focus to produce optimal results. You have to be present, truly immerse yourself into the Mudra practice and then....most wondrous things happen. Mudras take charge and you can follow your hands and experience the true depth of these ancient codes. Suddenly your soul power unlocks and is set free, your life perspective changes and you understand and perceive this earthly experience in a deeper, more profound way, all the while with a healthy distance from challenging times and expanded understanding of fortunate ones.

Each lifetime seems to have a hidden pendulum that swings back and forth, it seems there is an invisible balance that remains, no matter how it all appears to others from the outside. There is an order, there is a purpose and there is a designated path that each one of us is on, but all of our life's mysteries cannot be revealed at once. We must remain attentive in the present, the now, to truly experience every nuance that this earthly incarnation offers to teach us. If we understand and respect the pendulum, the balance will remain intact. If we fight it, it will be thrown off.

The inner balance is the true key to be able to journey thru life with enduring vigor and loving generosity while surrendering the final outcome to the invisible universal power that resides in us all. We must trust this universal navigation, for it knows us better than we ever will. It loves us more than we ever will. And it has a better plan for us than we could ever imagine. Mudras are one of these sacred keys, for they are connected to your every move and every breath. Understand them, use them, and let them serve you on your way to enlightenment, self-realization, healing, and the absolute fulfillment of your optimal potential.

As always, I remain eternally grateful for being given the opportunity to be the instrument for the transmission of these sacred teachings to you.

One in Spirit, love, and Peace. Blessings to all,

Sabrina

The History and Art of MUDRA

Hand gestures have been native to every culture on earth and can be seen as intrinsic to civilization: Ancient Egyptians, Romans, Greeks, Persians, Aborigines in Australia, ancient Indians and Chinese, Africans, Turks, Fijians, Mayan cultures, Inuit, and the Native American nations all used hand gestures.

Today, we still use hand language. Think about the universal handshake – a sign of friendship and peace. Applause is the language for approval and enthusiasm; the pointed index finger is used to scold; an upraised hand with the palm -out signals us to stop.

There are many points of view regarding the development of hand gestures. Scientists have proved that even apes communicate with their hands and firmly believe that hand gestures were basis for speech. A blind child who has never been able to see will still clap his hands to express excitement and happiness. Many hand gestures are universal, dating back thousands of years. In Egypt almost five thousand years ago, hand gestures were performed in prayer rituals by high priests and priestesses. Sacred hand gestures were key to communicating with the gods, manifesting miracles, and connecting with the afterlife. Egyptians carved these sacred gestures in bas-reliefs on the walls of and inside the pyramids, and they became the basis for their hieroglyphs. From Egypt these movements and knowledge of their spiritual power and usage traveled to India and Greece.

In India, these gestures were named "mudras," a Sanskrit word, and they became an irreplaceable part of yoga, which aimed to connect the practitioner to divine and cosmic energy. Mudras became the essence of this divine communication in Buddhism and Hinduism. Buddhist priests developed the understanding of mudras still further and used them to close prayer rituals, a practice that has remained alive to this day.

Plato placed hand gestures among the civil virtues in ancient Greece, where there was a distinct classification of hand gestures into comic, tragic, and satiric. From Egypt and Greece, these hand gestures were brought to Rome, where they became intrinsic to popular discourse and culture.

In the reign of Emperor Augustus in Rome, performances of hand gestures in pantomimic dances were a great personal delight of the emperor. Competitions were held between the best hand – gesture dancers, and all Rome was split into factions about their favorites. The most distinguished performer was often called the Dancing Philosopher.

In the year 190, there were six thousand performers in Rome devoted to the art of hand gesture. Their popularity continued until the sixth century A.D. Sacred hand gestures were also used in religious practice among Jews. In various portrayals of Moses we can observe him using mudras with gestures of blessing, divine protection, knowledge, and receiving guidance from the divine.

In Christianity, mudras took on a less noticeable form. Stylized hand poses are almost always present in portrayals of Jesus, but most people were not taught the significance of these poses. So the people in Western cultures lost the awareness of the healing and sacred power of the mudras and used them more as expressive communication gestures.

In Italian paintings before and during the renaissance, one of the most common hand poses is that of the connected thumb and index finger. Its meaning is that the ego – the index finger – is bowing to God – the thumb – in love and unity. In popular Neapolitan use, that gesture is called the kissing of the thumb and finger – the sign of love. In secular portraits, that gesture translates into approval of love and marriage. Some Native Americans also used that hand gesture when indicating that they thought something was good and approved of it.

Another common gesture in religious paintings is that of the palm turned upward. This pose dates back centuries and signifies openness and inquiry. In this book, it is part of the mudra of asking for guidance, and it has a part in mudra for facing fear. When you ask the Universe to protect and guide you, the palm is held so that something can be placed in your hand – something can come to you. American Indians translated this gesture into: Give me!

A gesture in which the pointed index finger moves in a circle has a universal connection – specifically, "no" – rejection in Italian, native American, and Japanese cultures, among others. When the index finger is pointed but motionless in popular usage and in high Italian art, it means indication, justice, pointing something out (which has led to the actual name of index for the forefinger). It can also mean silence, attention, number, mediation, and demonstration. Native Americans were among the most famed hand – sign communicators, usually signing in front of strangers. Early white settles actually believed that the American Indians rarely used spoken language, since the settlers most often saw them using hand gestures that Europeans didn't understand. Later on, Native Americans would play a key role in communicating with hearing – impaired children.

In Mexico, hand signs are found in elaborate ancient carvings, and they are also painted on ancient Greek and Homeric vases and pottery writings. The Chinese alphabet actually originated as the depiction of hand gestures. There are many commonalities among the hand gestures of Native American, Chinese, Egyptian, and African cultures. I hope that archeologists, anthropologists, and linguists can eventually piece together how these universal gestures come to be used in such different parts of the world. Hand gestures are the mother of all communication and are supremely powerful. The art of mudra is divinely inspired: It enables us to communicate with the divine, develop and aspire to higher qualities, and keep a universally popular language. Mudra is our connection to the divine play of the cosmos.

The time has come to revive and appreciate the gift of mudras practice to utilize these efficient, powerful ancient techniques in your everyday life. Mudra can help you follow your dreams: Your life is in your hands. There are no limitations.

MUDRA FOR TRANQUILIZING YOUR MIND

THE PRACTICE OF MUDRA

INSTRUCTIONS FOR PRACTICE

WHERE DO I PRACTICE MUDRA?

To practice mudra, find a quiet, peaceful, and private place where no one can disturb you. If that is not always possible, you can usually practice most of the mudras that are unobtrusive just about anywhere.

HOW DO I PRACTICE MUDRA?

During the practice, it is best to sit in a comfortable position. You can sit on a pillow or blanket in a cross-legged position, or in a chair, but make sure your weight on both feet is equal. It is most important that you keep your back straight. Maintain a comfortable sitting posture that does *not* give you pain.

WHEN SHOULD I PRACTICE MUDRA?

You can practice a mudra virtually any time that you feel the need to connect with the energy that it gives you. If you are practicing a mudra for insight or to enhance your meditation, however, the easiest time to concentrate is in the morning right after you wake up or in the evening before going to sleep. You should never practice a mudra on a full stomach, because your body-mind's energy is concentrated in your abdomen. Your overall energy is slow and needs to be permitted to be unimpeded as it focuses on turning nourishment into physical energy. After a meal, wait an hour before practice.

HOW OFTEN CAN I PRACTICE MUDRA?

You can practice as many mudras a day as you wish, but to obtain the full benefit that a mudra can give you, you will want to establish at least one three - minute set time during the day in which to grow comfortable with your mudra.

To feel the benefits faster, I recommend that you practice the mudra twice a day, each time for at least three minutes. Select a mudra that addresses a problem you have or a quality you want to develop, and make it a point to practice that mudra every day.

HOW LONG SHOULD I PRACTICE A MUDRA?

Your should practice a mudra in the beginning for at least three minutes a day, but when you have built up your strength and ability to hold the mudra and evoke its energy, you can extend your practice to eleven minutes. Ultimately, you may want to build up your practice to thirty-one minutes a day.

Most of the mudras will give you immediate results, in the form of more energy, clarity and peace of mind, or insight. More challenging or entrenched problems, however, will require more discipline and perseverance in your practice. It will take a few weeks of practice for the mudra to come into full effect and help you feel a profound transformation that will eliminate or resolve your problem.

MEDITATION

There are many different meditative techniques. If you have not meditated before, the simplest way to begin meditating is to find a quiet place and sit comfortably. Bring your attention to your breath: Exhale and inhale slowly through your nose and concentrate on your breath as it travels in and out of your body. As you concentrate, allow the awareness of your breath to still your mind and relax your body. You have begun to experience the essential state of meditation.

Meditation will lower your body temperature, so, when you plan to meditate for longer than eleven minutes, you should cover your back and shoulders with a shawl before sitting down. With mudras and proper breathing, you can achieve deeper levels of meditation. You will experience peace, relaxation, rejuvenation, and higher levels of consciousness.

Your intuition, patience, and wisdom will increase greatly, as will your personal magnetism and level of energetic vibration.

BREATHING

Proper breathing is essential when practicing a mudra. There are basically two types of breathing:

In **LONG DEEP BREATHING**, you take your time inhaling and exhaling slowly and completely, through your nose.

When you inhale, relax your abdomen and expand the chest.

When exhaling, deflate the chest and pull in the stomach to help expel the air. This technique of breathing will help you relax, calm down, and be more patient.

In the **SHORT BREATH OF FIRE**, inhale and exhale through the nose at a much faster pace. Focus on your navel point, expanding for inhalation and contracting on exhalation. Both parts are equal in time and can be quite rapid: two to three breaths per second.

This technique has a more invigorating effect.

Both techniques are very cleansing and healing.

During your mudra practice, it is best to use Long Deep Breathing except where noted.

CONCENTRATION

While practicing any mudra it is important to concentrate on the energy center of your Third Eye, which is between your eyebrows. Your Third Eye is the point of your body-mind that connects most easily to the higher sources of energy within you and around you.

As you practice meditation and mudra, if your mind wonders, gently bring your attention back to your breath and your mudra. Breathe in and out. You will experience a very powerful effect, a heightening of energy, throughout your entire body. Mudra practice affects each individual differently at different times. Sometimes you may feel a slight tingling sensation in your hands and arms; at other times, you may experience a sudden rush of energy through our spine. Allow yourself to feel and notice whatever comes up for you. Concentrating on the different feelings, allowing them to be there, will magnify the healing benefits to your body, mind and spirit.

Your Third Eye center is the point between the eyebrows.
By focusing your mind's attention on this energy center of intuition,
you can practice visualization and receive guidance and visions.
It is your window to infinite possibilities.

EYE MOVEMENTS

The eyes are an important element in the practice of mudra. How you use them will increase your concentration.

You can keep them half open and gently direct them to look over the tip of your nose. Do not cross your eyes to do this. Just look down and slightly in so that you perceive the end of your nose. This is a very beneficial exercise for your eyesight.

Another practice is to close your eyelids and gently aim your eyes upward toward the area of the Third Eye. If you need to keep your eyes open as you meditate, look into the middle distance and relax the eyelids. Most important, the eye focus should always be done *gently*. Never force your eyes into a painful or uncomfortable position.

VISUALIZATION

We all know how to daydream. Actually daydreaming is a form of visualization. In your mind you can create a picture, world, or dream in which you desire to live. Visualizing where you want to be and how you want to live and manifest your energy is the first step toward making your dream a reality. Mudra practice can help you actualize your dreams. The power of your mind is limitless. Live it, breathe it, and you will make it a reality.

For example: While practicing a mudra for anti aging, visualize in your mind a healthy, youthful glow around your face. See yourself and your face vibrant and recharged. By adding the power of your mind to your daily practice of mudra and visualization, you will change and improve your outlook, your energy, and your entire life.

As another example, when practicing a mudra for insight, see yourself as having reached a happy solution for a problem you've been trying to resolve. Visualize how you would feel if your concern were over. From this visualization will emerge a positive approach to creating a good outcome.

POSITIVE AFFIRMATIONS AND PRAYER

When you meditate, your mind becomes fine-tuned to your body's needs and you gain in healing capacity. It is important before you meditate to make a positive affirmation for yourself. You can also affirm positive energy for another person, just as you would in a prayer.

Example: When practicing the mudra for dieting it is beneficial to affirm:
"I am eating only healthful food. I am healthy, trim, and full. I am sticking to my diet."
This simple affirmation will have a positive effect on you.

When meditating or praying for someone else, it is helpful to see them surrounded by white or violet light and affirm: "My friend is healthy, happy, full of life, and smiling."
Your affirmation should always be formed in the resent tense. "I am calm," not "I will be or want to be calm." or, "I see the solution in my meditation." This positive statement creates powerful energy vibrations. Your energy is sent out into the Universe and manifests your desires and intentions, enabling you to accomplish your goals successfully, honorably, and compassionately. Prayer and affirmations are especially powerful during the practice of mudra when your mind is calm and your concentration is magnified.

MANTRA

While you may prefer to practice your mudra and meditation using your affirmation, you may also want to try using a mantra. Mantras are ancient Sanskrit healing words that have a powerful effect on your entire being when chanted repeatedly during meditation or mudra practice. The hard palate in your mouth has fifty-eight energy points that connect to your entire body. Stimulating these points with sound vibrations affects your mental and physical energy. Certain sounds that stimulate these points have a very healing quality. When you repeat aloud or whisper these ancient mantras or scientific healing-sound combinations, the meridians on your hard palate are activated in a specific order that re-patterns the energy of your whole system. There are three basic mantras that you will find in this book in different combinations:

EK ONG KAR
One Creator, God Is One

SA TA NA MA
Infinity, Birth, Death, Rebirth

HAR HARE HAREE
WAHE GURU
Hah-rah; hah-ray; hah-ree; wa -hay; guh-roo
God is the Creator of Supreme Power and Wisdom

Not every mudra practice requires a mantra. All mudras can be practiced in silence to the rhythm of your breathing. You can use the mantras when you are struggling with a restless mind, since focusing on the words will help center you. Follow your intuition during the mudra practice and if you are drawn to chanting the mantras, try them when you feel it is right. You will experience profound peace, joy, and passion. Your soul will sing with the Universe.

THE MANTRA PRONUNCIATION GUIDE

A like *a* in about
AA like the *a* in want
AY like *ay* in say
AI like the *a* in sand
I like the *i* in bit
U like the *u* in put
OO like the *oo* in good
O like the *o* in no
E like the *ay* in say
EE like the *e* in meet
AAU like the *ow* in now
SAT rhymes with "what"
NAM rhymes with "mom"
WAHE – sounds like wa-hay
GU – sounds like "put"
Emphasize the"ch" at the end of every " such."Pronounce the consonant v softly.
Roll the *rs* slightly. When chanting the mantra like " Haree Har Haree Har,"
make sure you do not move your lips, and pronounce it with the tongue only.

THE HANDS

Both hands and all ten fingers have individual, distinct meanings. Each corresponds to the energy of a different body part and to the energy of our solar system. The right hand is influenced by the Sun and represents the male side of one's nature. The left hand is ruled by the Moon and represents the female aspect of one's nature.

The right hand is the receiver while the left is the giver of positive powers. These meanings are also reflected in the hand positions of mudras.

Each finger is associated with a special ability, tendency, or characteristic and how it affects your life.

The **THUMB** symbolizes God. When the rest of your fingers connect to the thumb you symbolically bow to God. The Thumb is associated with the planet Mars and represents willpower, logic, love, and ego. The angle it makes with the rest of your hand when relaxed indicates your character. A distance between the thumb and index fingers of around ninety degrees indicates you are generous, kindhearted, and giving. A distance of about sixty degrees suggests a logical, rational character. A thirty-degree space indicates a secretive, sensitive, and cautious person. A long, strong thumb reveals a strong personality, willpower, and the ability to change your destiny.

The **INDEX** finger is influenced by the planet Jupiter and represents your knowledge, wisdom, sense of power, and self-confidence.

The **MIDDLE** finger is the indicator of the planet Saturn and relates to patience and emotional control. Therefore, it has a balancing effect on your life.

The **RING** finger connects with the Sun and represents vitality, life energy, and your health. It corresponds to your sense of family and matters of the heart.

The **LITTLE** finger is the indicator for the planet Mercury, which rules your ability to communicate, be creative, appreciate beauty, and achieve inner calm.

The tips of fingers can reveal qualities of different natures.

An oval fingertip can signify an impulsive person who needs motivation. A pointy fingertip is common for an independent, active person, and a square fingertip shows a logical and practical person.

THE CHAKRAS

Within our body, we have seven major nerve and energy centers that are located along the spine. The first is at the base of spine, the seventh at the top of the head. These centers are called Chakras. Their energy is always spinning clockwise within our bodies and influences - and is influenced by – our emotional, spiritual, and physical health. In order to feel balanced and in harmony within ourselves and our environments, it is important that we know about these centers and their functions.

FIRST CHAKRA
Represents: Survival, food, shelter, courage, will, foundation
Location: Base of spine
Gland: Gonads
Color: Red

SECOND CHAKRA
Represents: Sex, creativity, procreation, family, inspiration
Location: Sex organs
Gland: Adrenal
Color: Orange

THIRD CHAKRA
Represents: Ego, emotional center, the intellect, the mind
Location: Solar plexus
Gland: Pancreas
Color: Yellow

FOURTH CHAKRA
Represents: Unconditional true love, devotion, faith, compassion
Location: Heart region
Gland: Thymus
Color: Green or pink

FIFTH CHAKRA
Represents: Voice, truth, communication, higher knowledge
Location: Throat
Gland: Thyroid
Color: Blue

SIXTH CHAKRA
Represents: Third Eye, vision, intuition
Location: Third Eye
Gland: Pineal
Color: Indigo

SEVENTH CHAKRA
Represents: Universal God consciousness, the heavens, unity, humility
Location: Top of the head, crown
Gland: Pituitary
Color: Violet

CHAKRAS IN THE BODY
Base Chakra: Foundation
Second Chakra: Sexuality
Third Chakra: Ego
Fourth Chakra: Love
Fifth Chakra: Truth
Sixth Chakra: Intuition
Seventh Chakra: Divine Wisdom

Mudras are a powerful tool for energizing and balancing each Chakra, activating the electric current in our body, and releasing the limitless power from within. Example: When practicing the mudra for divine worship, you can visualize healing Chakra colors surrounding, filling, and energizing your body, starting with the First Chakra and continuing up to your head, the Crown Chakra.

ELECTRIC CURRENTS

Besides the seven Chakras within our body, there are seventy-two thousand electric currents or channels called *Nadis* - pronounced "nah-dees". They run from all different body points, from the tips of the toes to the top of the head. The Nadis also affect your entire system. Keeping these energy currents activated and full of powerful flowing energy is essential to your wellbeing. Each mudra redirects, activates, and empowers the energy flowing through those channels, and stimulates the brain centers, nerves, and organs, with benefits to your entire neuromuscular, physical, and glandular system.

HEALING COLORS

Using the healing power of colors can also enhance your mudra practice. The rainbow colors of the Chakras heal and reenergize corresponding body parts. You can surround yourself with appropriate colors whenever you meditate or visualize the colors as you practice mudras.

For instance, when practicing the mudra for powerful insight, you can visualize yourself surrounded by white or violet light. This will enhance your intuitive capacity. Wearing a certain color will also influence your entire outlook on life.

MUDRA OF YIN - FEMININE POWER

Examples:

RED will positively affect your vitality, ground you, and connect you to the earth.

ORANGE will empower your sexuality, creativity, and relationships.

YELLOW makes you feel energized and full of fire.

GREEN is good for the days when you need to heal your heart and feel love.

BLUE has a calming, peaceful effect on your aura or the energy field surrounding your body, and will help you see and speak the truth.

INDIGO will enhance your intuition and sixth sense.

VIOLET is a great centering and calming color that will help you connect with the universal healing powers.

BLACK will help you communicate as the leader.

WHITE will make you feel cleansed and pure, and will help clear you of any negative feelings or depression.

Reflect on the messages your body sends you every morning, and see what color you feel most drawn to and comfortable wearing on different days.

THE AURA

Our aura or energy body is made of electromagnetic energy vibrations that include color, light, sound, heat, and emotions. It surrounds us as a glow that is usually invisible. With practice and concentration, however, you can learn to see auras. The mudra for feeling the energy body is particularly effective in helping you discern auras. When our invisible magnetic force is very vibrant, it signifies good health, personal power, and a healing capacity.

USEFUL MUDRA TIPS

Some mudras may seem at first to be very similar to each other. Yet each is, in practice quite different: every detail in the posture of your hands and fingers is important and significant. When you pay close attention to your practice of mudras, you will feel the difference. As we discussed, every fingertip is connected to a different body center and energy current. Concentrate on the mudra as you practice, and notice the different feeling and effect that each brings to you. You can practice one specific mudra at a time or combine a few in one sitting. Listen to your body.

Example: If you are stressed out and need to concentrate, practice the mudra for preventing stress. After three minutes, go on to the mudra for concentration. As you try different combinations, your body-mind's logic and intuition will guide you. That is the beauty of the mudras – you can practice them anyplace, anytime, in whatever order you desire. This ancient science of the mudra is complex in benefits, yet simple in practice.

Now that you have some background about the power and history of mudras, and some rudiments of meditation practice, you're ready to begin trying some mudras and applying their energy to your life. In the next sections, you will find mudras for your soul, mudras for healing physical conditions, and mudras for easing troublesome states of mind, among others. Every one of these fifty-two traditional mudras can be a spiritual tool for you and help you in your own process of self-discovery and creative problem solving. I hope that they will enable you to find more insight, pleasure, and power on your life journey.

MUDRAS

MUDRAS
FOR YOUR BODY

YOUR BODY IS YOUR TEMPLE...
CHERISH IT.

This chapter gives you fifteen mudras that will help you calm, heal, and reenergize your physical body. An amazing and sensitive creation, your body needs loving care, proper food, and exercise. Appreciate, love, respect, and celebrate your body. With daily practice of mudras, you will learn to balance sexual energy, prevent aging and stress, conquer your addictions, physically relax, and recharge your body.

You can choose to practice only one mudra a day or as many as you wish until you feel energized, stress-free, and balanced. Be patient and practice self-love. See yourself with a healthy and vibrant body.

Mudra for Anti-aging

We all want to look young and healthy. A natural aging process is part of everybody's life, yet, no matter what your age, you can preserve and protect your body. Although a healthy lifestyle, with exercise and proper diet, is essential, the most powerful ingredient of an anti-aging recipe is a proper state of mind. With this mudra, you can cleanse all the impurities in your system, reverse the aging process, and learn to enjoy the wisdom and experience that you gain with time.

This breathing technique and mudra will cleanse and brighten
your aura and regenerate your cells, which will give
you a radiant face and prevent aging.

ÇHAKRA: Base of Spine - 1
Reproductive Organs - 2

COLOR: Red, Orange

MANTRA: EK ONG KAR SA TA NA MA
~ One Creator of Infinity, Birth, Death, and Rebirth ~
Repeat mentally with each breath

Sit with a straight back. Make circles with your thumbs and index fingers, and place the backs of your hands on your knees with palms up. Stretch the rest of your fingers out straight.

BREATH: SHORT, FAST BREATH OF FIRE, FOCUSING ON THE NAVEL. THE BREATHING SHOULD BE SO POWERFUL THAT YOU "DANCE WITH THE NAVEL." Practice for at least three minutes and relax.

MUDRA FOR STRONG NERVES

You can learn to remain calm and centered in your everyday life, even in times of challenge and turmoil. You will instantly feel the power of this mudra as if you were connecting two currents of energy, yet its effects are soothing and calming and will keep your nerves strong.

This mudra will strengthen your nerves.
By pressing the middle finger you are empowering emotional control,
and the pressing little finger activates inner calm.
Because female and male sides of the body correspond differently
in men and women, the pose is reversed for men.

CHAKRA: Solar Plexus – 3
Heart – 4

COLOR: Yellow, Green

Sit with a straight spine and lift your left hand to ear level, palm facing out. Make circle with the thumb and middle finger, and straighten the other fingers. The right hand is in front of the solar plexus, with the thumb and little finger touching, palm facing towards the sky. The rest of the fingers are straight. <u>The position of the hands is reversed for men</u>: The right hand is held at ear level, with the thumb and middle finger held in a circle and the left hand in front of solar plexus with thumb and little finger touching.

BREATH: INHALE IN FOUR COUNTS AND EXHALE IN ONE STRONG BREATH. Continue for a few minutes.

MUDRA FOR PROTECTING YOUR HEALTH

In addition to eating a proper diet, observing good hygiene, and getting regular exercise, you can preserve and protect your health by practicing this ancient and powerful mudra. Daily practice over many years will provide many benefits.

This mudra balances the distribution of red and white blood cells,
and defends your overall health.

CHAKRA: All Chakras

COLOR: All Colors

Sit with a straight back. Bend your right elbow and lift your hand up and out to the side as if taking an oath. Hold the first two fingers straight together and pointing up. Curl the other two fingers down into the palm and lock the thumb over them. Hold the left hand in the same mudra with the palm toward your chest, the two outstretched fingers touching the heart. Make the outstretched fingers as straight as possible to create a strong electromagnetic field around you.

BREATH: TWENTY SECONDS INHALE, TWENTY SECONS HOLD THE BREATH, TWENTY SECONDS EXHALE. Pull the navel in as much as possible on exhalations. Continue for a few minutes and relax.

MUDRA FOR PREVENTING STRESS

We all experience stress in our lives. Many of us run from one activity to the next, taking care of too many things in a day without finding enough time to recover. It is very important for your body-mind to give it times in which it can slow down. Practicing this mudra for a few minutes, especially when we feel stressed out, can help. You will feel the results immediately and may find that you want to practice this mudra daily to build your energy for keeping stress – free.

*This mudra enables the brain to maintain its equilibrium under stress
and keeps the nerves strong.*

CHAKRA: Solar Plexus - 3

COLOR: Yellow

Sit straight. Relax your arms, bending your elbows to bring your forearms in front of you and parallel to the ground. Bring your hands, palms up, to meet in front of you, about one inch above the navel. Rest the back of the left hand in the palm of the right hand. Keep the fingers straight and together.
BREATH: LONG, DEEP AND SLOW. KEEP YOUR MIND FREE OF THOUGHTS. Repeat for three minutes and relax.

MUDRA FOR HEALTHY BREASTS AND HEART

Our bodies have great self-healing and disease-preventing capacities that work best when we use our consciousness to activate, utilize, and strengthen them. Mudras help the flow of electric currents within the body to keep you healthy and vibrating with healing energy. In addition to any spiritual practice, every woman must perform regular breast self-examinations and stay in tune with her body, but this mudra will help the female system use energy to clean out the lymph glands in the upper chest, which preserves breast health. The heart muscle is working constantly, so we must help it recharge and get some rest.

This mudra will cleanse and recharge your chest area with self-healing energy. Daily practice will keep the heart strong.

CHAKRA: Heart – 4
COLOR: Green

Sit calmly in a comfortable posture, back straight. Relax your arms at your sides with the palms facing forward. Then alternately bend each elbow so that the forearms come up toward the heart center as rapidly as possible. When your right hand is at your chest, the left hand is away from the body, and when the left hand is at your chest, the right hand is away from the body. Do not bend the wrists or hands and do not touch the chest. Continue at a rapid pace four times while you inhale, four times while you exhale, until you feel hot, then relax for a few minutes.

BREATH: LONG, DEEP AND SLOW.

MUDRA FOR FEELING YOUR ENERGY BODY

The physical body is surrounded by an invisible energy body, or aura. With training, you can learn to perceive this vibrant halo that surrounds you. As you practice this mudra, breathe and concentrate, and you will begin to sense, see, and feel your energy passing between your palms. Regular practice will increase your ability.

By directing the palms and their auric energy glow toward each other, you magnify the energy field and can therefore perceive it more easily.

CHAKRA: Third Eye – 6

COLOR: Indigo

Sit with a straight spine. Bring your palms in front of you so that they are open and facing each other. The fingers are slightly apart and slightly cupped. The tips of the fingers are pointed away from you. Keep the eye focus between the palms. As you breathe, feel the energy flow from one hand to the other. After a few minutes, you will begin to see the flow of energy.

BREATH: LONG, DEEP AND SLOW.

MUDRA FOR PREVENTING BURNOUT

When you don't give yourself the proper rest that you need and deserve, you can endanger your mind-body health and drain your life energy. Whenever you feel so tired that it seems impossible to recover, this is the moment for gathering your last sparks of energy and practicing this mudra. Even if it is difficult to hold the mudra in the beginning, after three minutes you will feel rejuvenated and surprise yourself with the power that is within you.

The pressure of your fingers stimulates your electric currents
and recharges them with vital energy.

CHAKRA: Base of Spine – 1
Reproductive Organs - 2
Solar Plexus - 3

COLOR: Red, Orange, Yellow

Sit with a straight back, bend your elbows, and raise your forearms up and in front of you, parallel to the ground, hands meeting at the level of the heart, palms facing the ground. Fold the thumbs in across the palms of each hand until the thumb tips rest at the bases of the ring fingers. Keep the four fingers straight and together, face the backs of the hands toward each other and press only the fingertips together. Firmly press the fingertips and nails of each hand together, the upper hands not touching. Deeply inhale and completely exhale.

BREATH: LONG, DEEP AND SLOW. Repeat a few times and relax. Rest for a few minutes.

MUDRA FOR HEALING
AFTER A NATURAL DISASTER

Earthquakes, floods, tornadoes, fires and other natural disasters are unfortunately quite common. After such a traumatic upheaval, people feel disoriented, confused, vulnerable, and fearful. This mudra can have an immediate, powerful, positive effect and help you get through the aftermath of the crisis and realign your own energy with that of the earth.

This mudra will readjust the magnetic relationship of the two hemispheres of the brain, which will help you regain emotional balance.

CHAKRA: Base of Spine – 1
Solar Plexus – 3
Third Eye - 6

COLOR: Red, Yellow, Indigo

MANTRA: HARI ONG TAT SAT
~ God in Action, the Ultimate Truth ~
Repeat mentally with each breath

Sit up straight. Slightly cup your left hand and hold it over your left ear, keeping your left upper arm parallel to the ground. Make a fist with your right hand and extend your right arm straight out to the side, then bend your elbow so that your fist is by your ear, palm slightly away from you.

BREATH: LONG, DEEP AND SLOW. Continue for a few times and relax.

MUDRA FOR OVERCOMING ADDICTIONS

Addictive habits are a very common problem. All addictions are connected to our desire to avoid accepting that we are individuals responsible for ourselves. Our addictions let us feel less alone but also keep us from facing the reality of certain problems or situations. We try to alter our troubling moods and upset feelings by using addictive substances or distract our attention from ourselves with addictive relationships. To overcome an addiction, you must overcome the fear behind it. Distracting yourself with drugs, caffeine, alcohol, cigarettes, food, or bad relationships only worsens the problem. It also delays your achievement of your purpose in life. You can overcome any addiction; you just have to set your mind to it. The regular practice of this mudra for three minutes, three times a day will help you overcome any addiction in thirty days. Set yourself free from the chains of addiction and begin this practice of self-love today.

This mudra works on physical addictions as well as emotional addictions and codependence. The pressure of your thumbs on your temples triggers a rhythmic reflex current into central brain that balances the energies that cause addictions.

CHAKRA: Base of Spine – 1
Reproductive Organs – 2
Solar Plexus – 3
Heart – 4
Throat - 5

COLOR: Red, Orange, Yellow, Green, Blue

Sit up with a straight spine. Make sure you are not slouching, especially in your lower back. Make fists with your hands and then extend the thumbs out. Press the thumbs on the temples where you feel a slight depression. Clench your teeth, lock the back molars, and keep your lips closed. Vibrate the jaw muscles by alternating the pressure on the molars. A muscle will move in rhythm under the thumbs. Feel it massage the thumbs as you continue to apply firm pressure with them. Concentrate on your Third Eye center as you do this. Continue for three to eleven minutes. Now relax your arms and place them at your sides, with the thumbs and index fingers forming a circle. Hold the pose and relax. **BREATH:** SHORT, FAST BREATH OF FIRE, FOCUSING ON THE NAVEL.

MUDRA FOR HEALING A BROKEN HEART

When you are in the middle of grief and heartbreak, it seems pretty impossible to escape the experience. Sadness seems overwhelming initially, but with time you can come to understand why you had to go through that pain. Whatever the larger reason, while we are going through this painful experience, we can heal our heart faster with this beautiful mudra.

*This mudra is very relaxing and good for the nerves, and
it will calm and heal a broken heart.*

CHAKRA: Heart - 4
Throat - 5
Third Eye - 6

COLOR: Green, Blue, Indigo

MANTRA: HUMME HUM HUM BRAHAM
~ Calling upon Your Infinite Self ~
Repeat mentally with each breath

Sit up with a straight back. Hold the palms lightly together, with the tips of the middle fingers at the level of the Third Eye center. The arms are horizontal. Elbows out to the sides. Hold this mudra for at least three minutes.

BREATH: LONG, DEEP AND SLOW THROUGH THE PALMS OF YOUR HANDS, AS IF DRINKING WATER.

MUDRA FOR ELIMINATING FATIGUE

When the feelings of fatigue and exhaustion just overwhelm you, you can feel better with this simple mudra. Take a few moments to yourself, calm down, and breathe.

*This meditation will bring healing, boost your energy,
and enhance your intuition.*

CHAKRA: Solar Plexus – 3
Heart – 4

COLOR: Yellow, Green

Sit straight. Elbows out to the sides, hold your hands level, in fists, at the solar plexus, except for the index fingers, which are straight. Hold the right palm down, left hand palm up. Put the right index finger on top of the left index finger. The fingers are crossing exactly in the middle of the second segment so that a special meridian contact takes place.

BREATH: INHALE LONG, DEEP AND SLOW BREATHS THROUGH THE NOSE AND EXHALE THROUGH THE PUCKERED MOUTH SLOWLY, WITH FORCE, DIRECTING THE BREATH AT THE TIPS OF THE INDEX FINGERS. Meditate on the sensation of your breath on your fingers and continue for a few minutes.

MUDRA FOR DIETING

True beauty comes from the inside out. We each have a unique beauty, however, that is affected by what we eat. When we eat healthful food, we will have a healthful and vibrant appearance. If you crave junk food, this mudra will help you keep to you diet and curb your appetite, and it will still leave you feeling energized.

This mudra will build up your electromagnetic field and allow you
To draw energy from the Universe so that you can easily
maintain your body with less food.

CHAKRA: Base of the Spine – 1
Solar Plexus – 3
Crown – 7
COLOR: Red, Yellow, Violet

Sit with a straight spine and extend your arms out in front of you, parallel to the ground with palms facing up, hands slightly cupped. Very slowly move your arms back to your sides as far as possible, keeping them parallel to the ground with palms up. Then return your arms very slowly to their original position so that the sides of the palms almost touch in front of you. Repeat. Feel the energy coming through your Crown Chakra to your palms. As the palms come together, feel and resist the attraction. This maneuver builds up the energy in you. Continue for at least three minutes. As you need relax the hands in front of your chest, with elbows bent and palms facing each other. Keep the palms three inches apart and visualize a ball of energy between them. Continue for a few minutes and relax.

BREATH: LONG, DEEP AND SLOW.

MUDRA FOR RECHARGING

We all need to know how to recharge and rejuvenate our minds and bodies to keep up with personal and professional daily demands. You can practice this mudra anytime, and virtually anyplace. After just a few minutes you will feel a difference.

This mudra builds up energy throughout your system and gives you a greater capacity for dealing with life's challenges and tasks. The hands in this mudra activate and recharge the main energy channel in your spine, filling it with new vibrant force.

CHAKRA: Base of the Spine – 1
Reproductive Organs – 2
Crown – 7

COLOR: Red, Orange, Violet

Sit with a straight spine and extend your arms straight out in front of you, parallel to the ground. Make a fist with your right hand. Wrap your left fingers around the fist, with the bases of the palms touching, thumbs close together and extended straight up. Focus your eyes on the thumbs.

BREATH: CONTROLLED, LONG DEEP AND SLOW.

Continue for a few minutes and relax.

MUDRA FOR BALANCING SEXUAL ENERGY

We are constantly bombarded with sexual stimulants, distractions, and exploitations in commercials and advertisements. These images and attitudes actually deplete our essential sexual energy and make our sexual relationships difficult. Yet sex can be beautiful, giving, spiritual experience of two souls, which must be respected and cherished. During sex, a powerful exchange of two creative forces occurs that affects us for a long time, so it is most important that we keep our sexual energy balanced and nurtured. Negative past experiences can be healed and the ultimate sexual power and pleasure can be achieved when we consciously channel this energy.

This mudra balances and channels your sexual energy. It cleanses and recharges the glands that affect your entire sexual and reproductive system. For strength and confidence in your sexuality, the right thumb is on top of the left. For sensitivity and gentleness, the left thumb is crossed over the right thumb.

CHAKRA: Reproductive Organs – 2
COLOR: Orange

Sit with a straight spine, elbows slightly out to the sides. Clasp your hands together, interlocking your fingers. Leave the left little finger outside of the hand. By placing the right thumb on top of the left thumb we empower our masculine side, and when the left thumb is placed on top of the right thumb we recharge the feminine side of nature. Press your hands together in this mudra, hold for three minutes, and relax.

BREATH: INHALE AND EXHALE STRONGLY THROUGH YOUR NOSE.

MUDRA FOR LONGEVITY

With proper diet, exercise, and this ancient mudra technique, you can prolong life. Your body rhythm is the determining factor for your longevity, and this mudra taps into the energy of that clock and fine-tunes it. With regular daily practice for three minutes, three times a day, you will enhance and prolong your life span.

This mudra works on the life nerve, which runs along your spinal cord and helps create a new body rhythm, increasing your longevity.

CHAKRA: Base of the Spine - 1
Crown - 7

COLOR: Red, Violet

Sit with a straight spine and stretch your arms in front of you parallel to the ground with elbows straight. Palms are facing up towards the sky. Cup your hands together as if water were about to be poured into them.

Hold for at least three minutes and relax.

BREATH: SHORT, FAST BREATH OF FIRE, FOCUSING ON THE NAVEL.

THE SACRED MUDRA SEQUENCE
FOR MENTAL, EMOTIONAL AND ENERGY BODY BALANCE AND CLEANSE

This very specific mudra sequence is called Kirtan Kriya. It is an excellent and effective tool to cleanse your Auric field and bring the mental, physical and emotional body into a state of balance. The pituitary and pineal glands are stimulated, the negative thought patterns can be erased and a new balance is established.

MANTRA:
SA TA NA MA
~ Infinity, Life, Death, Rebirth ~

Sit with a straight spine and rest the wrists on your knees. If possible stretch your elbows. Close your eyes and mentally focus on the area of the Third Eye. You will be connecting the thumb fingertips with other fingertips in a specific order sequence, while repeating the mantra.

TIMING:

THE MUDRA MANTRA SEQUENCE IS REPEATED AS FOLLOWS:

3 MINUTES IN NORMAL VOICE ~ awake state, earthly realm, the world

3 MINUTES IN LOUD WHISPER ~ longing to belong

6 MINUTES IN SILENCE ~ divine infinity

3 MINUTES IN LOUD WHISPER

3 MINUTES IN NORMAL VOICE VOLUME

These three modes of chanting relate to three levels of meditation:
With regular practice extend each segment to 5 min. and silence to 10 min.
Upon completion of this meditation sequence, deeply inhale and exhale,
stretch your arms up, spread your fingers, breathe long, deep and relax.

FIRST POSITION:
Connect and press together the thumbs
and index fingers while chanting: **SA**

SECOND POSITION:
Connect and press together the thumbs
and middle fingers while chanting: **TA**

THIRD POSITION:
Connect and press together the thumbs and ring fingers while chanting: **NA**

FOURTH POSITION:
Connect and press together the thumbs and ring fingers while chanting: **MA**

MUDRA INDEX

ABOUT THE AUTHOR

SABRINA MESKO Ph.D.H. is a recognized Mudra authority and International and Los Angeles Times bestselling author of the timeless classic *Healing Mudras - Yoga for your Hands* translated into fourteen languages, as well as twenty other books on Mudras, Mudra Therapy, Mudras and Astrology, and meditation techniques.

Sabrina was born in Europe where she became a classical ballerina at an early age. In her teens she moved to New York and became a principal Broadway dancer and singer who turned to yoga to heal a back injury. She studied with Master Guru Maya, healing breath techniques with Master Sri Sri Ravi Shankar and completed a four-year study of Paramahansa Yogananda's Kriya Yoga technique. She graduated from the internationally known Yoga College of India and became a certified yoga therapist. An immense interest and study of powerful hand gestures - Mudras, led Sabrina to the world's only Master of White Tantric Yoga, Yogi Bhajan, who entrusted her with the sacred Mudra - hand yoga techniques giving her the responsibility to spread this ancient and powerful knowledge worldwide. She studied with him privately under his personal mentorship and guidance, and continues to teach Mudra techniques as taught by him.

Sabrina holds a Bachelors Degree in Sensory Approaches to Healing, a Masters in Holistic Science, and a Doctorate in Ancient and Modern Approaches to Healing from the American Institute of Holistic Theology. She is board certified from the American Alternative medical Association and American Holistic Health Association.

She has been featured in media outlets such as The Los Angeles Times, CNBC News, Cosmopolitan, the cover of London Times Lifestyle, The Discovery Channel documentary on Hands, W magazine, First for Women, Health, WebMD, Daily News, Focus, Yoga Journal, Australian Women's weekly, Blend, Daily Breeze, New Age, the Roseanne Show and various international live television programs. Her articles have been published in world-wide publications. She hosted her own weekly TV show educating about health, well-being and complementary medicine. She is an executive member of the World Yoga Council and has led numerous international Yoga Therapy educational programs. She directed and produced her interactive double DVD titled *Chakra Mudras* - a Visionary awards finalist. Sabrina also created award winning international Spa and Wellness Centers and is a motivational keynote conference speaker addressing large audiences all over the world. Sabrina recently launched Arnica Press, a boutique Book Publishing House. Her mission is to discover, mentor, nurture and publish unique authors with a meaningful message, that may otherwise not have an opportunity to be heard.

She is the founder of MUDRA MASTERY ™ the world's only online Mudra Teacher and Mudra Therapy Education, Certification, and Mentorship program, with her certified graduates and therapists spreading these ancient teachings in over 26 countries around the world.

WWW.SABRINAMESKO.COM

Milton Keynes UK
Ingram Content Group UK Ltd.
UKHW051335220823
427296UK00002B/18